Sovereignty

Will of man
Vs
Will of God

By: Tommy Loveland

Sovereignty will of man

The sovereignty will of man
Is within the very nature
Where we have fallen
Free will you say
Yes we are free
Free to love our sin
Our freedom has led us to slavery
And we claim to be sovereign

Through our fallen nature
We claim to be wise
but became fools
Given over to our sins
We do not seek God
We seek our sin
For that is the nature we are in
Our sovereign will

“as it is written: "None is righteous, no, not one; no one understands; no one seeks for God. All have turned aside; together they have become worthless; no one does good, not even one."”

Romans 3:12

Chapter 1: A clear vision

Let's start in the beginning:

The book of Genesis is the very first book of the Bible. Moses opens it up he says:

“ In the beginning God created the heavens and the earth.”

But if we fast forward to the new testament in the book of John,

John says this:

" In the beginning was the Word and the Word was with God and the Word was God."

And then it says this in John 1:14

"And the Word became flesh."

So you see in the beginning was Jesus and Jesus was with God and Jesus was God and Jesus became flesh.

In Hebrews chapter 1 it says this:

"Long ago, at many times and in many ways, God spoke to our

fathers by the prophets, but in these last days he has spoken to us by his Son, whom he appointed the heir of all things, through whom also he created the world. He is the radiance of the glory of God and the exact imprint of his nature, and he upholds the universe by the word of his power. After making

purification for sins, he sat down at the right hand of the Majesty on high, having become as much superior to angels as the name he has inherited is more excellent than theirs. For to which of the angels did God ever say, "You are my Son, today I have begotten you"? Or again, "I will be to him a father,

and he shall be to me a son"? And again, when he brings the firstborn into the world, he says, "Let all God's angels worship him." Of the angels he says, "He makes his angels winds, and his ministers a flame of fire." But of the Son he says, "Your throne, O God, is forever and ever, the scepter of

uprightness is the scepter of your kingdom. You have loved righteousness and hated wickedness; therefore God, your God, has anointed you with the oil of gladness beyond your companions." And, "You, Lord, laid the foundation of the earth in the beginning, and the heavens are the

work of your hands; they will perish, but you remain; they will all wear out like a garment, like a robe you will roll them up, like a garment they will be changed. But you are the same, and your years will have no end." And to which of the angels has he ever said, "Sit at my right hand until I make your enemies a footstool for

your feet"? Are they not all ministering spirits sent out to serve for the sake of those who are to inherit salvation?"
Hebrews 1:1-14

Jeff Durbin says it best –

"So Jesus upholds all things by the word of his power which means this that he carries the universe along to its intended destination."

So when I say let's start in the beginning I'm saying let's start with God.

Who is God?

God is Love!

And if God is love
then what does He love?
You cannot love
without an object to love on!

For example: If I say:

"I love!!!"

And you say:

"What do you love Tommy ?"

I'd say I love football!! That's the object I love it, I love football, I love my son he is the object you cannot love without an object to love on!
So how can God be love
if He is only one person?
And when we say God is love we mean that from all eternity.
The Psalmist says:

"From eternity to eternity
you are God."

You see- the Father loving the Son, the Son loving the Father and the Holy Spirit.. God is love! The trinity is the very basis for love!

Father

Son

Holy Spirit

One God

3 persons inhabiting one being

Not 3 gods not 3 beings

3 persons

One being

And we were created
in their image.

Now let's talk about our beginning? In the beginning God created the heavens and the earth. God said let their be light and theirs light, let there be fish in the sea and there is, let their be animals

among the inhabitants of the earth and there is. He creates what He wants He does what He pleases, He speaks and life is created and obeys. Then He creates man in his image. Now stop and think about that for a second? We are made in the image of God. We were made for His glory!! And God tells man

and woman dominate the world and inhabit it. Take dominion over it. You can have anything you want except the fruit from this tree!! Do you see our free will? Yep!!!! There it is free to choose and we chose to disobey, we were deceived and chose the fruit that God said we can not have. So what's the big

deal?? Big whoop!! We ate some fruit bro!! Chill!! Well let's talk about the fruit. What is this fruit God says we can not have? What's the big deal? Why put it there in the first place? It's just fruit! Let me take you away from this scene and bring you to something we create and understand how it works, like a

car every single part or piece of a car helps it run the motor the oil and gasoline every piece is very very important and if somebody came up to you and asked you:

"Hey bro why aren't you putting milk in that car?"

You would say:

" Because it takes gasoline dummy!" (haha) That's what makes it run that's what makes it work. And when God made the world He put a tree there and this tree contain fruit(Gods fruit) and it wasn't just any type of fruit it was a special fruit and this fruit contained the

knowledge of good and evil. Wow!! Think about that now?? Knowledge of good and evil! Yep! What's wrong with the world today? You have every image bearer of God with the knowledge of good and evil. And every image bearer of God is professing their knowledge of good and evil. And as you can see my

knowledge of good and evil might be different from your knowledge of good and evil or from the atheists viewpoint of knowledge of good and evil or the Muslim his knowledge of good and evil or the Jehovah witness their knowledge of good and evil or the Mormon their knowledge of good and evil or the

Buddhist their knowledge of good and evil or the Hindu or the surfer dude, The NFL superstar, The famous musician, the politician or military person... and so on and so forth I think there's like 400 billion different world views out there. That was a joke but the point is everyone has a world view and

everyone is professing their world view. But what's God say? That's mine if you take it you will surely die! Understand this when we stole the knowledge of good and evil and we use it for our own agenda death enters the world sin takes control we now have fallen away from God into the very nature of sin we love

our sin we worship our sin we want to be the sovereign we want to be the one over the knowledge of good and evil and it's in all of us every single one of us!

And when we say:

"But I have free will?"

You see that very nature come out of us, we want to be sovereign!

Now I know what all you image bearers are saying right now that if you don't have free will then how am I making my own choices? But I'm not saying you can't make choices

you can do whatever you want inside the nature you are in. See Jesus says things like this:

"No one can come to me unless the Father who sent me draws him. And I will raise him up on the last day."

John 6:44

Jesus also says:

"If you sin then you're a slave to sin but if the Son sets you free you will be free indeed!"

When did we ever get the idea that we're free?-Jeff Durbin

And Jesus also says that we have to be born again?
(In John chapter 3)
Then He says whoever believes will have eternal life. So you have to be born again first then you believe. So you see what's really happening is it's God who seeks not man. If a

man is seeking God it's because God sought them. And some of you might disagree or say no it couldn't be that way! But if you say that don't you hear your own sovereign voice? Are you the sovereign? Or is God the sovereign? You see , you will hear a lot of Image bearers say they have

free will? But think about this? Does God have free will? In psalms 115 it says God is in the heavens and He does whatever He pleases. If God has free will and man has free will and God freely chooses to save you because He loves you, let me ask you a question? Who can stop the free will of God? Did

Lazarus argue with God when Jesus raised him from the dead? Nope!! Jesus said Lazarus come out and a dead man walked out of the tomb. If God says let there be light...there's light! He speaks and all of creation obeys! So again we are free but only inside our nature where we haven fallen and a dead

man can do nothing! It's all about God! He is sovereign and He declares the end from the beginning. God is good! And His will is Good! Every choice He makes is the best choice. I hope this is humbling you cause if it's doing anything else to you than your not getting it, and that's ok when God

moves He moves and if you're his sheep then you love Him and He loves you and that's all that matters. This knowledge doesn't save you, only Jesus saves and Jesus is God in control of all things. Read your bibles and the words will jump off the page at you of God's sovereignty.

Chapter 2 is some poems/writings shedding light on what I've been talking about so far.... Sovereignty. Some of them might be hard to understand so if your not getting it that's ok just move onto the the next one when you get into chapter 3 it

will all come together. Thanks and enjoy!

Chapter II : Submission chamber

The sovereignty will of man

The sovereignty will of man
Is within the very nature
Where we have fallen
Free will you say
Yes we are free
Free to love our sin
Our freedom has led us to slavery

And we claim to be sovereign
Through our fallen nature
We claim to be wise
but became fools
Given over to our sins
We do not seek God
We seek our sin
For that is the nature we are in
Our sovereign will

Admonition

I have discovered by it's very sound we fall, by it's control we worship, by its very command we follow and obey. The knowledge we contain is in all of us letting us know that the clock is ticking and time has become our god.

Love

Love has always existed it has no beginning it has no end it is always perfect the very basis is it's being inhabiting eternity.

Love created you and me and all that we can see love is perfect and love is all we need.

A relationship with love
leads to eternity
Everything else is
temporary and meaningless
The temporary things
lead to no where
The meaningless things
lead to death

If you do not have love
you have nothing

Love is the Father
And the Father loves His Son
And the Son loves His Father
And the Father loves the Spirit
And the Spirit loves the Father
and the Son

God is Love God is One

Dead men tell no tales

I can't escape this knowledge
Every where I turn it pulls me a little closer
Every step I take is another step closer to you
I feel the curse within
The black sails of of my soul
Dragging me down to the depths
To the bottom of the sea floor

I should of never eaten the fruit
That led me to depravity
A rebel soul
Just another casualty
Dead inside a tomb

Inside the abyss

Dead men tell no Tales
And lose lips sink ships

The condition of man

If God were to look into the future
and see who would choose Him all
he would see is a graveyard
With our middle finger pointing to
the sky!
That is our condition
And what can a dead man
do?....Nothing

gods

I'm on top of the mountain
I'm the king of the earth
I'm a god spitting laws
Ever since my birth
I'm the sovereign
I make my own way
Yea I'm the king
Doing as I please

Commanding everything
To bow down to me
I soon found myself
Found myself in chains
As my sin led me to a dream
A dream that I'd be king
Of neverland

Said the death machine

Rebel soul

Now Love moved
And spoke to me
With my fist in the air
As I lie beneath
On the ocean floor
You resurrected me
You loved me
You wash me

And made me new
You saved this rebel soul
That once hated you
I could not resist
Your love is to great
My eyes were open
to your mercy
And how brand new it is
Every morning

Your grace is overwhelming
Like an ocean overflowing
My spirit seeking Truth
An eternal debt I owe to you
But you paid it
through your blood
Amazing Love
As an eagle seeks to fly
Souring the beautiful blue sky

A second death I wait to die
As my soul awaits
For eternity

Testify

I speak to people
all day long
Telling them about my savior
They laugh at me
they spit in my face
But when Love moves.....
What can a dead man do
But be resurrected
And seek the Truth

Sovereign

When God moves there is not a maverick or molecule, height nor depth, angel or demon, creature on earth or in the deep blue sea, or in life or in death, or all eternity that can stop Him!

He does whatever He pleases!!

I did not choose to be here

I don't get to choose
when to leave
I did not choose to pick Him
I did not choose to believe

He chose me
He died for me
He saved me
He resurrected me

He loves me

And now I believe and seek Him

Transcendent

Life is beautiful
Even in the darkest times
The only thing that's tragic
Is the nature
we have obtained
And until our eyes are opened
From the idols we proclaim
This pain is here reminding us
That our hands are in the flames

Not of this world

I went to a cemetery today
And I listened to those
who have no choices
I sat and eavesdropped
On those who have no voices
But all I heard was
The wind blowing
And birds chirping

The silence of the voiceless

The peace of nothing
Not a word was said
It stirred my soul within me
The light began to shed
And I come to realize
Within the civilized
That I was living among the dead

Sovereignty of God

God is love

God loves His Son

God is in control

Knowledge cannot save you

Only Jesus saves

Jesus is Lord

Lord over all

Repeat !

Chapter III: Will of God vs will of man

"For I am not ashamed of the gospel, for it is the power of God for salvation to everyone who believes, to the Jew first and also to the Greek."

Romans 1:16

The gospel is the power of God
for salvation!

The gospel is the power of God
for salvation!

The gospel is the power of God
for salvation!

The gospel is the power of God
for salvation!

The gospel is the power of God
for salvation!

The gospel is the power of God
for salvation!

The gospel is the power of God
for salvation!

The gospel is the power of
God for salvation, salvation

doesn't come from anywhere else! Not my unique taste in music not some fancy church not how I dress not from any ufc fight night or super bowl party not some sort of clique and not from our works! It's the gospel! I can't say it enough the gospel is the power of God for salvation!! It's good news that Jesus

is King it's good news that Jesus is our savior it's good news about God's grace and His mercy! Jesus is Lord and He is Lord over all!!

He does not need your permission to be Lord

He is the Lord.

And He is over the

Knowledge of good and evil!

And what do we do with this
knowledge?
We display it daily!
And my knowledge of good and evil
might be different than your
knowledge of good and evil.
Everyone in this world
has a world view.

Everyone! Everyone stands on a platform and professes what they believe and what they think is right or wrong every one has a system of ethics. Now that doesn't mean everyone has thought through their worldview? But the point is everyone has the knowledge of good and evil.

For example:

Black lives matter
Abortion is murder
White people are evil
America is evil
America is good
Religion is what's wrong

with the world
Islam is the only way
Christianity is the only way
Jehovah witnesses is the only way
Mormonism is the only way
Their are many ways to heaven
Their is no God or heaven or hell
Judaism is the only way
(the chosen people)

Buddhism is the only way
Their is no good or evil were just
matter in motion
Should I keep going??? Woo!!.....
Scientist and their study's show
how we came about and our
knowledge of good and evil is a
result of brain gas??!!
(Wow? That's a good one!)

and on and on we go!!
How bout this one : whatever
culture you come to their belief in
good and evil is different
from the next?
China has their system of beliefs on
good and evil
America has theirs

England has theirs
And so on and on and on......
Get the point?
Everyone has the
knowledge of good and evil!
Everyone stands on a platform and
professes it.
Especially a famous artist
Watch this :

I'll just list some famous quotes/ movies/ tv shows/and some bands for an example
And by the way I'm not hating on these bands or movies I love music and movies and I think they are awesome in their gifts and talents to perform/entertain but anyways just an example and you can use this on

any artist or person or belief system or what ever.

Each of us has a vision of good and of evil. We have to encourage people to move towards what they think is good... Everyone has his own idea of good and evil and must choose to follow the good and fight evil as he conceives them.

That would be enough to make the world a better place.

-Pope Francis

The power of choosing good and evil is within the reach of all.

-Origen

No man has a good enough memory to be a successful liar

-Abraham Lincoln

We must reject the idea that every time a law's broken, society is guilty rather than the lawbreaker. It is time to restore the American precept that each individual is accountable for his actions.

-Ronald Reagan

Education without values, as useful as it is, seems rather to make man a more clever devil.

-C. S. Lewis

Life is tough, but it's tougher if you're stupid.

-John Wayne

Movies or Tv shows or how about just the news it's in all of them here is a small list

Star Wars
Star Trek
Die hard
Tombstone
Avengers
Harry potter

Lord of the rings

Guardians of the galaxy

Batman

Spider-Man

God Father

A few good men

Cinderella

Aladdin

24

Greys Anatomy

Law and order....and so on!!

Wooh!! Should I keep going or just say all of them how about music I'll least a few...

Pantera- mouth of war

Metallica –Enter Sandman

Lincoln park – crawling

Rage against the machine – know your enemy

Eminem-not afraid

Cypress hill- how I could just kill a man

Limp Bizkit – my way

Lady gaga- born this way

Taylor Swift – bad blood

Adele – Hello

Bon Jovi- wanted dead or alive

AC/DC - Hells bells

Johnny Cash- ring of fire

Tim McGraw-humble and kind

Phil Collins-I wish it would rain down

Elvis Presley- Devil in disguise

Ok if I keep going this book would be very very very very long and have to list every song/movie from everyone but the point is it's in all of us it's in our songs our movies our video games , TV shows, the news, it's on social media, it's in our schools, in the work place, on the playground, in our government and the military, its in our churches, on the streets, everywhere we go it's in all of us

and we profess it daily our knowledge of good and evil. We claim to be sovereign and we follow people in herds from what they profess. But what does God say that He is sovereign and He's the one that's over knowledge of good and evil not us! We have to give up self-righteousness we have to give up our sin and rebellion towards a holy God we have to be born again and that only

happens through a sovereign and a holy God!! His will not mine my will leads me to a graveyard and God's will leads me to paradise and saves a wretch like me.

Knowledge of good and evil, it's in all of us we're guilty as charged, it doesn't belong to us! We are fallen! We are all in a fallen nature worshiping what we say is right or

wrong! We claim to be sovereign and there is the problem that exists in the world. So what's the solution? We'll we can't just stop using the knowledge of good and evil it is in our nature it's what we do! Well we have to die and be born again and take on a new nature! We must first repent of our self righteousness our

indifference our claim to fame our sins that defy and rebel against a holy God. And the only way if that's going to happen is if the One and only sovereign God wills it. We talk about our free will to much.
Almighty God has free will to ya know! And His will is sovereign! He declares the end from the beginning!

He raises the dead to life! And our nature as fallen image bearers of God has to die and be raised to life again born again with new life in Christ with the new nature that God is sovereign and I'm not. That is the solution. Christ upholds all things by the word of His power He brings dead people to life He takes

a heart of stone and turns it into a heart of flesh like Ezekiel 36 says, whatever He says whatever He commands He has authority He is sovereign! God is all knowing He doesn't have to think about something like we do He knows it and He declares it!

Jesus says this to a Pharisee He tells a Pharisee who's really smart in the Scriptures very intelligent he knows the Hebrew law he knows his Torah he knows his Tanakh (which is the Old Testament scriptures) and he asked Jesus

"Tell us if you're the messiah stop beating around the bush just tell us plainly ?!!"

Is basically what he says to Jesus,

" Just tell us plainly if you are the Messiah!!"

And I love Jesus's answer but first let me tell you what He does not say, He does not say....

"Oh wait you missed the message?? Oh yes I'm the Messiah!!"

Or He doesn't say .....

"Oh you missed the sermon?? Well I'm sorry that you missed it! Maybe you can catch it on my youtube channel or fb live?!"

(haha)

No He does not say that at all!!

He says this: ...

"I told you!!"

"My sheep hear my voice and you are not of my sheep I lay my life down for my sheep and they follow me!"

I used to once think that I had free will and God was waiting for my invitation to make Him King and Lord of my life and God has shaped my heart here lately because no one makes Jesus Lord!! He is the Lord and He is Lord over all!!

He sits enthroned
at the right hand of the Father
His will be done on earth
as it is in heaven
no one can stay his hand
and say what have you done
He is Lord
Lord over all!!

He is our God in the heavens and He does whatever He pleases
All life in heaven and on earth was created to glorify Him!
It's always about Him and the day we make it about someone else or something else is the day we create an idol and make it about ourselves.

"The human heart
is a factory of idols
And it is never idle
it's constantly making them"

-John Calvin/Jeff Durbin version

Oh and I'm not a John Calvin fan
either don't know much about him I

just agree with that quote. But I am a huge Jeff Durbin fan and one of my heroes of the faith!

"The heart is deceitful above all things, and desperately sick; who can understand it?"
Jeremiah 17:9

"All these evil things come from within, and they defile a person.""

Mark 7:23

Jesus says there's two people one built his house on a rock the other one built his house on sand and then a great storm comes and beats against both houses the one on the rock survives the one on the sand is left in great ruin its fall is great and Jesus says if you don't

build your house on the rock of His word you're on sinking sand.

Jesus says there's two people there's two paths there is two gates and two destinations.

There is a path that leads to heaven and there is a path that leads to hell one person goes to

heaven the other person goes to hell wide is the gate in the path to hell narrow is the gate in the path to heaven

Jesus says there is 2 people
There are 2 paths
There are 2 gates
There are 2 destinations

Your are either in
Adam or in Christ
Your are either
Fallen or redeemed
Your are either
on the Rock
or on sand
Your are either
for God

or against God
You are either
saved or lost
Your are either
blind or you see
You are either
a sheep or a wolf
You are either
worshiping your sin

Or you're fighting
against your sin
You are either
Dead or Alive
Jesus says there's 2 people

Always 2
Which one are you?

The Bible is a story Gods story and we are in the middle of His story. Lucifer was an angel in heaven and free and he rebelled against God and was thrown out of heaven onto the earth and is no longer free but has taken on a nature of sin and he is a slave to sin.

God created man in His image and man was free and man was tempted and deceived by lucifer better known as the devil or satin and we sinned against God and now we are a slave to sin and death enters the world and man now has the knowledge of good and evil and we worship this knowledge we create

our own laws to survive as slaves to sin. Understand this God did not create Adam and Eve and then hand them the Ten Commandments and say :

“here ya go! Now if you don't follow these rules your out of the garden and you will surely die!”

That's not what happen, we're told not to touch the knowledge of good and evil! That's it one rule! And we disobeyed God and we're deceived and stole the knowledge of good and evil. We claim to be sovereign over this knowledge and our sovereignty takes us by our hand

and leads us to our own grave! We cannot contain this knowledge it belongs to God and God alone. But now that we have this knowledge then God comes in and gives us the Ten Commandments and His laws....why? So we can follow them? Don't make me laugh bahahahaha!!! That's impossible! If

that were the case then what's the need for Jesus? Gods law is a mirror to show you and me how corrupt we are and that we need a savior! So watch this God says He is over the knowledge of good and evil so when He gives us the Ten Commandments it's not for us to follow because knowledge of

good and evil belong to Him. What's really happening is He is preparing the way for His Son. And Who is The Son? He is God! And God who is love and if God is love what does He love He loves his Son. The Bible is Gods story the Old Testament is the records of fallen man and fallen

angels and both are slaves to sin both have a nature of death and the Old Testament prophesies are about Gods Son and He will bring a kingdom and salvation for the image bearers of God not the fallen angels God has already spoke of the fallen angels and there future and where they are going. And the

New Testament is about Gods Son and He speaks to us and commands us to repent and believe in the Son or you will perish in your sins. But how can a dead man fallen in sin come to God? God calls, God saves, God redeems, God forgives, He does whatever He pleases. God loves His Son and

the Son becomes flesh and dies for our sin He takes our place on that cross He absorbs Gods wrath for our sin He destroys death and is resurrected on the third day and sits at the right hand of the Father and the Father puts His enemies under His Sons feet and He calls. That's where we are today! Jesus

brought the kingdom as planned on time with Him on earth and if you are born again if you are raised to life in Christ if you are pursuing Jesus then you belong to the kingdom of God. And it's beautiful! Gods story! It's always about Him He brought His kingdom and it is one not of this world. God

commands the ones that He called to go get His sheep so that none are lost!! And He will not lose one of them!! The cross is a salvation that saves that truly saves 100%! God loves His people and He will go as far as the curse of sin is found and until there is no more and His enemies will be a footstool for His

Sons feet and then He will return... It's God's story and He saves His children and He does whatever He pleases.

The Rising

I was brought up in church had christian parents who raised me right and lots of christian friends learned a lot about the bible but never ever did I question it's foundation or search through it for

myself. I did not like church, to be honest I hated it, my parents made me go to church. I didn't want to go, I thought the lessons were corny some of my teachers were cool others not so cool but I did have fun but something was stirring inside of me, I didn't want to be at church and honestly if I could have my own

way, I would not go to church and my rebellion began all I thought about was myself what can I do for me. I got into lot of trouble when I was a kid things my parents and friends don't even know about and I'm kind of afraid to record it in this book (haha) I remember stealing things, lying, cheating , I could not

wait to get out on my own. And like any teenager I started smoking and drinking- why? Cause it was fun! And this led to marijuana and lots of bong hits!! Then to lsd better known as acid or tripping, there was one time I had a bad trip I took to much acid and smoked a lot of weed and then all of a sudden I remember

I had to go to the bathroom and when I went into the bathroom I don't remember using the bathroom but something crazy happened I felt like my soul came out of my body and I walked into the other room where all my friends were and none of them could hear me none of them could see me and I was talking to

them but they ignored me they didn't know I was there it was almost like I died and came out of my body it was trippy!! But then all of a sudden I came back to and I'm still in the bathroom and my hands are on the sink locked down tight and my face is about 2 inches away from the mirror and I'm looking dead into my

own eyes and when I come to it really freaked me out and if you done acid before then you know what I'm talking about having a bad trip the rest of the night was horrible I didn't think I was gonna make it through the night I thought I was gonna have to go to the hospital or even worse that I was

going to die! I remember praying to God and telling him I would never do drugs again but that didn't stop me after I made it through that I started using cocaine and sometimes a combination of different drugs. I remember a few times inhaling freon to get high??!! How the heck am I still alive???!! I

did whatever to get high or wasted! I've been in a bad car wreck due to drugs and alcohol that split my head wide open, I've been to jail. It led me down a dark road of rebellion which then led to crime I've set cars on fire destroyed property broke into cars and stole things... so on. I got in trouble with the law, I stayed

in trouble, and constantly lived my life on the run trying not to get caught! I partied hard fell in love with heavy metal music I love heavy-metal music I love the lyrics I love the guitar riffs I love the drums and the beats I love the bass, basically heavy-metal became an idol. And I still listen to heavy-metal to this day

I still love metal but I don't worship it like I used to so please don't think that I'm saying don't listen to heavy-metal heavy-metal is cool dude!! But anyways, while I was high on drugs broke as a joke my family and friends constantly told me about Jesus and I didn't want to hear that!! A matter of fact I made fun of

Jesus I even got into a very very very bad habit where I would use the Lords name in vein on purpose because that's what rebels do we defy a Holy God we raise our fist in the air and we say no not your way my way!! But one day I remember my sister telling me about Jesus and I remember telling her

that she did not realize the things that I've done I can't go back to God I don't want to get in trouble because I knew deep down in my heart I knew God and was resisting Him but at the perfect time in the perfect moment God moved and His love I couldn't resist, He made me alive!! He forgave me of all my

sins!! I was dead in my sins and trespasses loving my sin worshiping my sin I was dead and God raised me from the dead born-again new life! I see sin now how it truly is before I did not see sin this way, sin is the enemy, sin leads to death, sin separates us from God, sin is a lie from the beginning that we're

sovereign over the knowledge of good and evil and we worship this knowledge. Anyways something happened that day that night I gave my life to Christ it wasn't me something else was at work in me the Holy Spirit convicting me drawing me to Jesus and the Father drawing me to his Son Jesus!! I felt like

God let me taste a piece of heaven. Out of all the drugs and partying I've done I've never felt so alive! His peace is like a drug I crave! It felt so good to be forgiven and know that He loved me. I remember picking up a Bible that night and when I opened it up I was in the book numbers reading about Moses in

the desert and the Israelites were sinning and God sent poisonous snakes to kill them for their wickedness but then God told Moses to make a bronze snake and put it on a staff and raise it up in the air that anyone who was to look at the staff would be saved from the poisonous snakes and this story

kind of freaked me out cause I was actually looking around the room thinking a snake was going to kill me for my wickedness haha! But I could relate to the story I did feel like I was in the desert I did feel like I was being attacked by snakes and I did feel deep down that I needed to be saved! But I didn't totally

understand this story it was a little strange so I flipped the Bible from the Old Testament to the New Testament one flip and now I'm in the book of John, chapter 3. Now growing up in church I knew a very popular verse in John chapter 3 John 3:16 which says:

“for God so loved the world that he gave his only son that who so ever believes in him will not perish but have a eternal life. But as I looked down the first thing I saw was John 3:14-15 you know what John 3:14-15says:

"Just as Moses lifted up the snake in the wilderness, so the Son of Man must be lifted up,"
"that everyone who believes may have eternal life in him."
John-3:14-15

I gave my life to Christ right then and there! Redeemed born again

new life new beginning Christ as my God and over the knowledge of good and evil. He is sovereign and He is Lord over me. And the Lord who is Sovereign over all is the greatest treasure any one could ever receive!! His will not mine! Because His will is perfect His will is Sovereign.

I've learned a lot about tradition especially in churches and the main thing they do teach correct is that Jesus is the only way and that He is the only one that can save you. But sometimes we get lost in where somebody says things that doesn't line up to what God says, and we

as christians have to know what God says about Himself, because sometimes christians they get duped they get things twisted sometimes they believe what somebody else says on tv who is popular or on the radio or some song or piece of music or a book or from a friend and sometimes we make things up

through our feelings which is very dangerous or wherever and it spreads like wildfire and we have to be careful not to try to defend things like tradition or other image bearers of God who have the knowledge of good and evil and are professing something they heard or felt. What does God say?   Read

His word and obey it God is sovereign He declares the end from the beginning and in order to do that you have to be outside of the beginning and the end He is eternal He inhabits eternity there's nowhere in this universe that you can go and God not be there!

The Psalmist says:

"If I go to heaven you're there if I go to the grave you're there to!!"

God is everywhere inhabiting eternity and He's sovereign. And if you're His sheep He says He's going to get you I hope this book

touches your very soul and that the Holy Spirit convicts you! Jesus says He lays his life down for his sheep and they are in His hand and nothing can snatch you out of His hand and He (Jesus) says and I am in my Fathers hand and no one can snatch you out of my Fathers hand and Jesus says I give them eternal

life and they follow me. The rising of His kingdom is reigning now Jesus died for our sin and was buried and rose again on the 3rd day and now He sits at the right hand of the Father and God is placing all of His enemies under His Sons feet and He calls everyone to repent and believe! That's the call, to

turn and believe, come to Christ for forgiveness and salvation!

Jesus says:

"Truly, truly, I say to you, whoever hears my word and believes him who sent me has eternal life. He does not come into judgment, but has passed from death to life."

John 5:34

Special Thanks

My wife Christy you are my backbone and I am so blessed to live and share my life with you! My daughter Sarah and my son Andrew (The best kids ever). My Mom who raised me right and I'm so

blessed to have an amazing mom(Love ya mom!) My Dad who is with the Lord and taught me everything I need to know , my sisters Cathy (well I have to say my favorite sister!), Susan (well I have to say my favorite sister!) and Becky (well I have to say my favorite sister!) (ain't nobody

chasing me boy!! Haha only they will get this?? :) My awesome brother-in-law's Dave (The man), Jeff (my fishing partner!!) and Brandon (Xbox Madden Champ!!
Haha!) Also Tony and Sandy Michael and Lily Damron (you guys are awesome) Walter and Renee (love you guys) and their

kids Walt and Josh(oh yea Josh W. I let you beat me in madden haha!!)   my nephews Josh Senesac (Xbox I will beat you in Halo one day!!) and Jessica, Hunter and Chase! Frank and Carrol Vallencourt (thanks for everything you guys are amazing!) The Vallencourt family who gave me an

opportunity! (Mike and Cathy Vallencourt Mike Jr and Daniel Vallencourt!)

Coot, Edwin, Clyde, Ryan, Will, Donnie S., Donnie C., Adam, Marcus, Stan, Steven, Josh, Paul, Greg, John Boy, Rocky, Mark G., Mark Willie(my nag) and all of Vcc!! The Loveland Family

(Uncle Tommy, Uncle Johny, Uncle Gary, (3 amazing uncles!) Michelle(love ya) Victoria(love ya) Julie, Laurie, Misty, Gary John, Aunt GG(love ya) Uncle Dick and Aunt Barbara (Love you so much) Denise Bremer(love ya cuz!) Lori Bremer, My Awesome Cousin Richard Bremer and his

amazing family(love ya bro!) Andrew Schwab and Project 86,Payable on death (pod) Demon Hunter, Living sacrifice, Jeff Durbin and Luke Pierson (some of my heroes of the faith!) Apologia church, The whosoever's, My church family RCC,The Queens family, The Westfall's, The Carlton Family,

The Woods, and everyone else I did not mention love you guys!! And most of all my Lord and Savior Jesus Christ who raised me from the dead and is sovereign!! Sovereign over all!!

www.ingramcontent.com/pod-product-compliance
Ingram Content Group UK Ltd.
Pitfield, Milton Keynes, MK11 3LW, UK
UKHW041945190726
13854UKWH00004B/1797